INTO THE
ELEMENTS

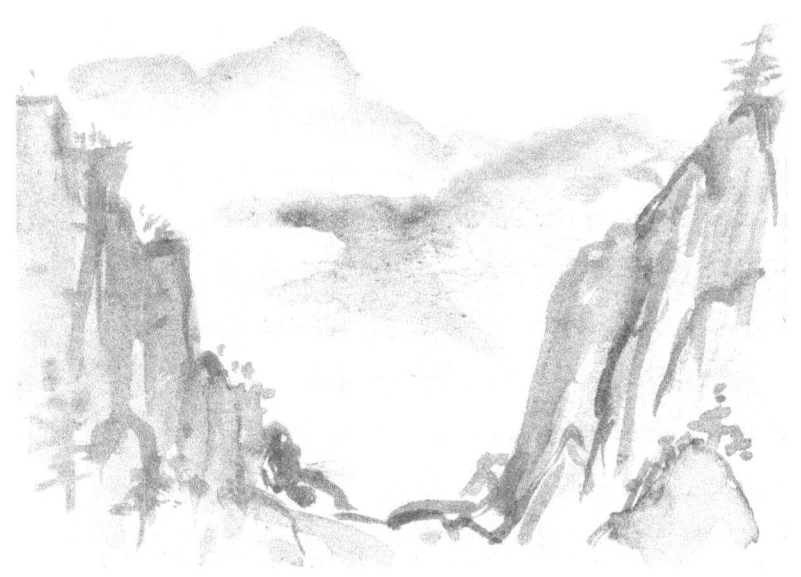

Poems by Irene H. Wellman

Artwork by Tara Marvel

Acknowledgements

"Then I Returned to the House of the Slow Letting Go" appeared online in *Streetlight*, 2017

"In the Space of Time" and "The Wright Brothers" appeared as prize-winners in *The Poetry Society of Virginia* annual poetry contest

"Vision" published in *Rattle*, 2015

Printed in June 2024
Artwork by *Tara Marvel*
Graphic design by *Stefano Buro*

ISBN 979-8-9908698-0-6
Into the Elements © Copyright 2024 by *Irene H. Wellman*
All the images are copyright to their respective owners.

Ash Haven Books 2024

For my granddaughter,
Ayla

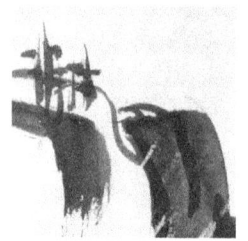

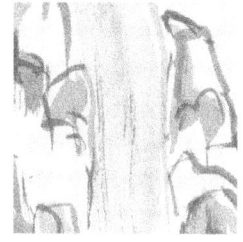

Contents

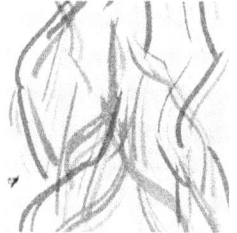

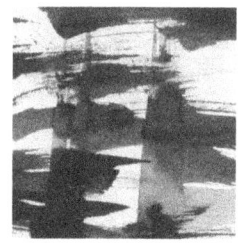

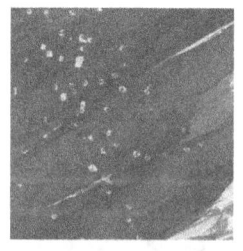

Introduction

Please enjoy these poems and their embrace of the five natural elements: Earth, Water, Fire, Air, and Space, with artwork rendered by Tara Marvel. The impetus for this volume was a reading for the Vespers Poetry program of the First Unitarian Universalist Church of Detroit. I am grateful for their steadfast championing of poetry in this community and beyond.

My thanks go to those too-many-to-name who have provided me much support and encouragement. My particular gratitude goes to Anne Gautreau and the Dearborn Writers Group, to WriterHouse in Charlottesville, VA, with its spin-offs, including Keep Writing Virginia, and to my writing group in New Hampshire. Last, I give thanks for Bill Plyler's and my family's support as I continue my writing journey.

EARTH

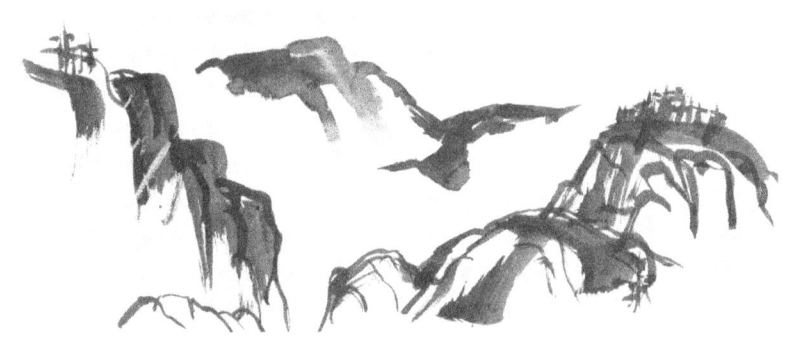

Vision

Where the tree limb was cut
an eye
looks at her,
the eye in the forehead
that remembers other lives,
looking back down a long tunnel,
death before death,
birth before birth
to the first,
the essential
One

who foretold her,
saw her here
from the pupil formed
by the cut of an axe.

She sees it watching her,
then shifts away.
The eye knows her, met her
when she was the size of a fist,
and before, the length of a leaf,
and when she was the speck of an atom
twisting in the vast blue,
and before,
fire and dust
arisen from unsteady waves of space,
even when nothing could escape,
no light or flame.

Yet between herself and the eye
is all that has happened—
the tree, the axe,
the reason for cutting,
a sharp separation,
the scent of cut wood.

It was Nothing Really

A storm had passed.
I stopped the car to walk
up and down the country lane,
woods shadowing the horizon.
New leaves, wild flowers,
water on the road.

A few cars passed.
Then the sun's rays scattered out
under ranged clouds, etching
each rain drop on the leaves,
each leaf, each twig,
each small stone, stiff petal,
each distant tree, near tree,
rivulets of bark.

Every moment grew longer,
drawn out farther
into a wide circle, and yet
close as veins on a leaf,
glittering.

When I left at last,
swinging out onto the highway,
the faces of the people passing
arose like blossoms
out of the dark.

Sycamore

This sycamore survives everything:
fire, floods, wind, pestilence, age,
at least for another year,
lifting its bones to the sky,
waiting for spring
to push up its sap,
make new leaves
as big as a hand slap.

I pull off a seed ball, a whole globe
packed on its surface with tight brown seeds,
a multitude of seeds to spread
across the earth.

This tree I return to is not mine
though I call it mine.
It stands apart,
catching the ropes of the air.
I too stand my ground,
watch its stubbornness, its cast-off limbs,
indifferent to dogs and walkers.

In summer, I hear
it rustle to the river,
bird song imbedded in its canopy.
I see how it strips
its bark back white,
to let in the rain and sun.

I wish I had its sure sap,
the clear streams of its heart.

The House of the Slow Letting Go

The house stood filled with the presence
of the dying man. It was his garden
he'd brought back from wildness, tended
with the dry warmth of his hands.

I went out into the evening,
walked alone with my clippers
to dead-head the marigolds,
the peonies no longer spinning planets,
the brown-leafed rhododendrons.
I picked up my watering can to slake a thirsty fern,
pulled aromatic leaves off the pink geraniums,
surprised a brown thrasher in the grass.

Above me, the two green ash trees,
one male, one female, swayed
towards each other over the house,
closing their eyes to the wind.

The Center

The center
of life, child,
is like the inside
of a daffodil.
The center will be open and flared,
will summon you with the trumpet's shout,
will point you in, guide you
to the stamens where
the pollen shines,
honey can gather on your tongue,
and everything is gold, gold, gold.
Go there.
Renounce the easy things.
Enter.
Then come away with the full nectar.

Change

change the flush of apple blossom
time's hand upon its fading brow
life's span this flood from then to now

twisting what's given, braids of sea
dandelion chains of time-turned sun
upon the tolling backs of waves

the fire inside the sweet embrace
washes away all death can bring
remember this, remember this

and in the end, remember this
how apple blossom softly rained
into a green and peaceful dusk

WATER

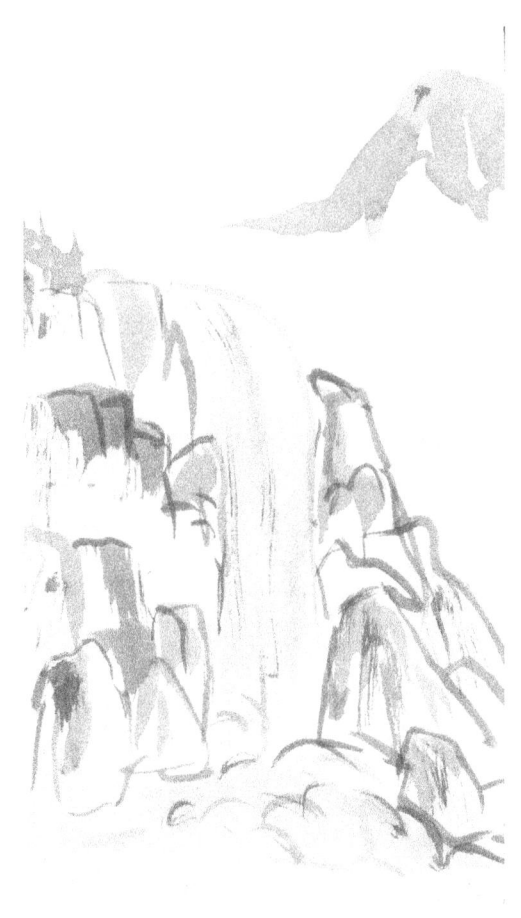

Momentum

I am
in this moment
that keeps going over
the edge,
disappears and is replaced
just as suddenly by another
until I am completely
fooled.

But I have caught some moments craftily.
I have several of them
stashed away like tissues in my mind
in case someone else
should die
and I can use them
to dry my tears.

Herringbone Sky in Southern England

A wide shallow sea
mirrors sandpipers,
sea glass, sandworm spirals.

My actress grandmother in nubbly swimsuit
wades slowly out,
loose skin spiny with goose bumps.

Resigned to old age,
she lets herself in and swims,
one arm over the other,
pointing hands and feet.

After youth, success, acclaim,
a daily ritual
on the only stage.

She emerges, rises, tall,
toes splayed
on firm sand.

She always held my hand
down the stone pier steps
on the gray edge of the waking town
and told me,
"This is how you hold your back straight."
"This is how you fall."

Rain Memories

My mother has buttoned me with her into her raincoat.
A spring downpour.
Her cotton dress cool against my back,
her silk scarf tickling my neck,
I peep out at the world.
I'm safe in this makeshift tent,
her voice vibrating against me.

Today, we walk together down the lane.
I stop to wait for her.
She points with her walking stick
at the darkening sky.
At the pond, flag irises reflect.
Frogs feel our tread on the bank and leap.

In the Space of Time

The woods, newly abandoned by glaciers,
hold hollows filled with marshes.
Red-winged blackbirds crack the air with calls,
silver-backed turtles bask on striated rocks,
water lilies fold like books,
and if you're lucky, at dusk, a soft-treading moose,
glossy in summer coat, dips his mouth.

Here my daughter ran from morning to night,
echoed the running river with her laughter.
In winter, we walked between lacy hemlocks
sticky with resin sap after snowfall, and slid
to the very center of ice-bright lakes.

Now, her wedding dress, scuffed from the dance,
lies crumpled on my closet floor,
the mask she wore of make-up and teased hair
washed off.

She has gone like a heron
beating its wings
down the river.

Some Day Emerging

May I wake to the world whole again,
rise from fitful sleep
to the sunlit garden, acorns
knocking on my head as I walk
    through leaves that lie
        like prone lovers,
            open and fearless.

All insights forgotten in the bell-blaze of oaks,
    knowledge erased,
        vows broken.

Because being human
all we have is hope
to be scattered among the hungry
    or long buried
        and found again
            under last snow.

Emerald Pool

You step into the coldness
of Emerald Pool,
feet, legs, flinching stomach.
Water tickles your navel,
rises to your chest,
until there's nothing for it
but to
plunge.

In an instant, skin is numb.
You feel voices summon you,
through far northern forests
out onto half moons
of pure beaches,
into the sea.

But you must surface or die.
You breach into sun, shadows
of pines, silver birches
scrolling off their bark,
and high above, the waterfall
suspended in time
over rocks and moss.

Pine scent crackles in your nostrils.
Bird calls. Laughter.
Skin jumps.
You're awake.

FIRE

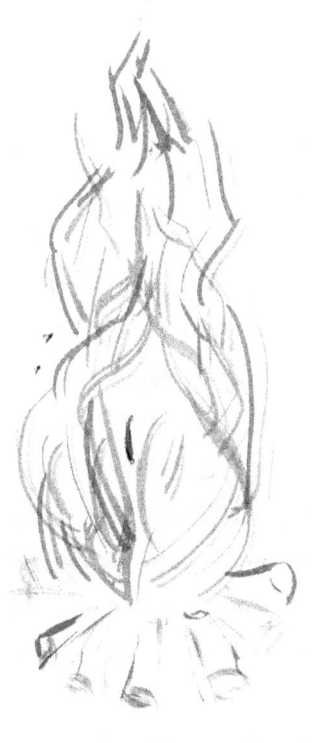

Old African Knife
(made for my parents during fieldwork, circa 1953)

The blade struck long ago
by Chikasa, the village blacksmith,
was forged in a charcoal fire
blown hot with bellows
until the flames grew orange,
and the long iron glowed.

Hammer rung on steel on anvil
in rhythmic measure.
Slowly its form emerged,
beaten to the thickness of the spine.

Blue-black oxide scale scattered,
peacock colors bloomed,
as he turned it over to find
its suppleness,
striking the steel to sharp-edge,
dipping it in quenchant.

At last, flame-hardened,
stroked to smoothness
in the bellow's blast,
tempered from brittle to tough,
he carved its handle
of the brown-grey wood of a ritual tree.

Once it opened
an antelope's belly
to its coiled entrails,
slashed a rubber tree
to press out sap white as breast milk,
cut out the hard stones
of red fruit,

and after forest fires
bit off singed leaves
in the smoky morning.

So it got bent from wear
and was brought away
and found in my mother's kitchen drawer.

Now hammered straight again
it hangs on a wall for viewing,
far from fire.

To the Sun

There you go, Sun,
falling over the Shenandoah Valley
as if this view of distances
can't hurt me,
and I won't remember
I've been here before when he and I
took pictures of each other
and walked the narrow path around,
as if he hadn't lost his hair and beard
and all was well in the autumn light
you shed on each twig
of twisted mountain trees.

A sudden gust came then, as now,
and you set, as you do,
too slowly for patience,
filtering through cloud layers.

But really it is we on Earth who are rising and turning
to leave you, and you stand still,
it seems, despite your breathless balance
on the galaxy's fingertips.

Time means little to you,
who's seen it all, as we
try to hold on to the remains,
and yet still leave too soon,
getting back in the car, plowing
into the night,
while behind us, you burst out, shouting,
"Red! Purple! Magenta!"

A Quiet Day

What begins in the morning sun
Lighting this side of the house now,
Rainbows on the walls,
Mountains swaying through the window,

You, grandchild, will see,
Will be a new growing star
Will draw a thousand rainbows
Across the sky's patient canvas.

Your mother holds you now
As if in her hands she holds rainbows,
As if she walks across the mountains
Carrying hope.

So I hold my love for you as a rainbow
Passed carefully to light another,
Afraid to let the flame blow out
And all stars be extinguished.

To My Young Poet Self

On rereading the first line of my first real poem.
"When the sun awakes with a flashing golden eye."

Today, I wake early to dawn, sun flashing through stark trees.
A sparrow chirps as I open the front door.
My bare feet slip on the frost-slick deck.

It's the same sun I woke to long ago,
as if Caedmon sprang from a dream, and sang,
hearing the heavy throated chant, swelling cry of the choir,
the black bull's roar as he pawed
the grass in a spring field,
bathed in the cadences of folk and high language.

Later, came Shakespeare's comedy and tragedy,
Tintern Abby Wordsworth, Keat's fluting nightingale
that I too heard once in London alley.
Then, the voices of America,
thump of drum and zing of fiddle,
the Irish woman keening a ballad
of burning beacons on cliffs sending farewell
to those who must leave their land,
and bass, baritone, tenor, alto blues
of people beaten and enslaved,
the soprano soaring above calling,
freedom, freedom, freedom.

Years have passed since that first poem.
Today, my young poet self and I
awake to the sun and its flashing golden eye.

Perspective

Van Gogh learned perspective,
where the vanishing point lies,
only the horizon
to obscure our view,
yet we search ahead
for what waits beyond.

His sunflowers burst
out of the canvas, blasted
by thick brushstrokes
until they engulf our eyes,
flames from a sun storm.

Yet towards the end,
Van Gogh painted himself
in flat madness,
no protrusions, only surface.

His stars swarm overhead,
pierced by church spires, cypresses,
omens of what is to come.

In his last painting, distance comes so near,
we step back,
find no room to breathe, battered
by the blood-black wings
of crows, chaff, and flying seed.

Angels

Over wars, angels hover
beating their trembling wings.
You cannot see or hear them.
their faces turned aside,
coiled hair raised
at the cries of innocents
that rise like arrows to pierce their chests.
Beyond the blue-black of space
They sing songs of pity,
mouths heated with radiation
for children wrapped in shrouds.
Unheard, their feet drum in pain,
and in the pupils of their eyes
is chaos.

Let us pray to them—
Michael, Gabriel, Raphael, Azrael—
as their shadows fall on ruin, rubble, flames,
as they pass over us, glinting with gold of frescos,
growing symmetry in the hands of sculptors,
flying down from stained glass windows.

Here on earth
may we, at last, see them,
as the dust of guns and bombs
clears for an instant
now and at the hour of death.

AIR

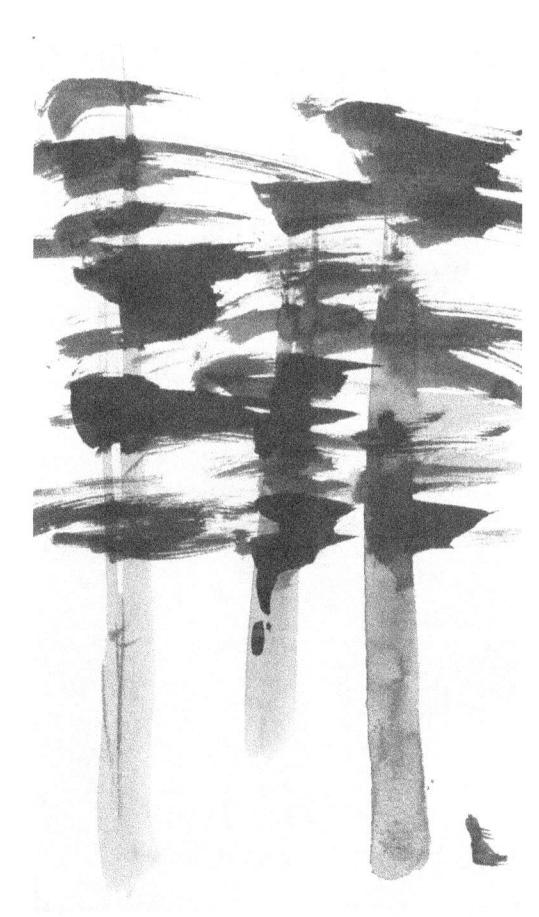

Wind Storm

Wind chivies the stiff hands
of the leaves as it crosses the grass.
Along the path, the daffodils fray
their faces on the earth.

Willful trees
muddle their branches, randomly
drop dead sticks,
rattle as if dying.

Our great green ash
grapples the sky,
its open nakedness
crucified in every blast.

We humans have no place here.
Hair raised at the howl
riding the valley, we lie
under layers of blankets and watch,

in penetrating cold,
the sky gather its forces.

Kite Day at Nelson County

It tugs, erratic at first,
a clumsy rainbow unable
to get free of the earth.
Down it dips, obedient to the invisible
strength and pull of its string
and the wind's spin,
impossible to predict—
heat, field, mountains.

But my hand unravels its puzzle.
It's so high now, it does an arabesque,
solemnly turning its face,
a stained glass brilliance,
to the sun.

Then it must fall
to wait, outstretched on the grass,
for me
to release it again.

Fall Thoughts

Sun pierces slate-grey clouds
and fires up a burnished maple.
Then rain sweeps the leaves away.

I can't keep up
with this temporality,
its flight that won't wait for me,
skeins unraveled in rolling umbers.

I'm pushed
into wind tunnels of trees.

I'm a child who still
escapes into air.

History won't remember me
and few of us who run here,
unable to bind up this gold.

Triptych for Trains

I.
You know that moment when you fling up the window
and you're on a curve, the engine coming into view ahead.
The whistle blows, your hair whips against
your face, the sharp wind takes your breath away,
fields, cows, birds seem to be flying, everything
louder, brighter than you expected
you know that moment.

II.
I'm a little girl of ten,
wearing a dress my guinea pig peed on this morning,
my fingers sticky with sweets I found in my pocket,
my bare knees goose-bumpy cold.
The steam smells like ironing, drops of rain on my cheek,
bits of coal spinning past the open window
foxgloves on the banks swaying
to the breeze of the passing carriage—
foxgloves safe and sweet
as mother's hug and father's shoulders,
as the floor wiggles under my lace-up shoes
and the steam puffs like clouds
to the sound of rhythmic clatter,
sudden confusion of rails, then
slowing.

III.
A long delay on a train to Washington, already night outside.
But now the whistle never stops blowing in its hurry
to make up time, or maybe for fear of killing lovers
caught on the tracks on this warm spring night
as memories leap
in the lonely whistle and romance of fellow travelers,
black windows pierced
with lines of frantic lights.

The Wright Brothers Museum

The hand-crafted engine parts
and the wings' sailcloth, clean and white,
sewn on their mother's sewing machine.
Maple seed shapes of ailerons
for right and left and lift.
Two simple huts to live in,
three stone markers for each new flight,
the one hill beyond,
circled by paths and pilgrims.

The older men
stop to look
with the intent faces
of many men I've known,
tinkering with bikes,
chains, wrenches,
pumps and tires,
finding yet another way
until they could
coax the wind,
free-wheeling,
to let them go at last
into lighter air.

Nash Point, Wales

I stand in a gale on a cliff.
Below, they have gone down the steep path to the shore,
but I know I can't follow, must stay put.
The wind buffets my face,
my white hair grows wild.
I become the grass
as it bends to the ground with each gust.

I give up resisting, as I must,
boundaries, edges gone.
How much have I
held tight?

The gale refuses
to accept this shell I inhabit,
opens me to grass seeds,
cracks in the rocks,
clouds' brokenness.

In song or prayer, I hear
an Aeolian chant.
Now I know nothing but
the wind.

SPACE

Perseid Meteor Shower

Standing on the sand
in summer in Canada at 3 am, I find
the Milky Way strung overhead,
white line
of receding breakers.

All my camera can collect
is the tide foam
and lamps of cabins.

I am precarious
with no anchor
except a few rocks.
I have swung out
into space.

Look, a shooting star,
white as acid, a homesick traveler,
come from an unknown place.

I too could fall
farther into this darkness
and be swirling
ashes among rocks,
a light soon extinguished.

The Struggle to Write

May begin on the quilt-crowded, unmade bed,
people waiting, dogs curled with glassy eyes,
grey limbs of oaks, shadowy in the fierce sun.
Time grips with tight teeth,
bodies appear at the door, dreams bark,
but the pen is already sinking
into the paper, a submarine
nosing lantern-eyed monsters,
tips of sea mountains,
volcanic black-gold flames.
And now it breaks surfaces, rises
into flocks as they swing and spread,
a monarch butterfly feast, a flash
of rainbow grackles, a turmoil of clouds.
The waiting left behind,
gone in an instant
another illusion,
only words now in a water-flow sprung
from this spring.

Box Turtle on Display

He has tried
all four sides of his cage,
pushing his head
between the wires, even climbing high
until he fell on his back, death to most turtles,
but scrambled upright
on tortion legs.

His red eyes beseech.
A box turtle
needs to roam the grass,
doze in the shadows of a bush.
I want to free him
but he's been rescued
from an abandoned basement,
could never find his natural home again.
So I stare back at him, transfixed,
caught like him against my will.

I touch his four black claws,
his orange plated carapace,
smooth head. He might live
a hundred years like this,
but now he searches his small world
for a hole, a break in the bars.

Until he stops to sleep,
inert as a rock, eyes open,
neck still stretched forward,
an innocent man in a cell,
brow pressed against a wall.

Trenton Railway Station-

Fall rain sweeps the steps as I enter.
An old black man sits on a bench
bundled in a down jacket, frayed pants, worn sneakers.
a walker against his knees.
Sometimes he sleeps. Sometimes
he stares at the floor. Then I see
he's wearing a woman's pink woolen hat.
Who left him there? Dressed him?
Undresses him?

Around him, people come and go.
Business men discuss the best resort,
a fashionable couple clicks by,
others pace back and forth in the shoes
of the homeless and hungry.

I'm hungry and find the station food-stand,
an echoing place, people hunched
over distant tables.
I order a sandwich, but leave one half.
As I throw it away, a young man
comes out of nowhere, cries, "Wait! Wait!"
thrusts his whole arm into the bin,
spinning greasy paper into space,
but too late, the box of food has dropped
beneath his reach.
He curses, turns, and wanders off
while I call out,
"What have I done? What have I done?"
No one answers.

Waking at 2:53 am

Is my old boyfriend's father dead?
All I remember is that in Great Neck, NY,
he passed by me in the kitchen,
then balding and energetic.

I have this memory as if
etched in clay, cannot imagine
time has taken him and put him in the grave,
mourners under umbrellas.

That boyfriend now may have grandchildren,
perhaps with red hair, just like him.
He's lost his parents, no doubt
remembering when dirt hit the coffin.

Memory, like amber,
is fixed in the mind
down to the last detail
a wing edge about to fly.

Faces distorted by the sun
or camera, one eye shut, a loose mouth,
the wrong or right angle,
my granddaughter climbing a tree.

This generation moves together
day by day, a slow train
of snapshots, snuffling, shuffling,
creaking across high bridges.

Mountains that arose in the distance
come closer. I can capture
grains of gravel seared by the heights,
icy snow even in summer.

At the summit in the young air,
a moment spliced like a drink of pure water,
we rest, looking down
at the chasm below
and the long descent.

Sound Waves

Without my hearing aids
sounds escape me-
running water, bird song,
words, phrases, whole sentences.
My ears hear soft static instead.

Across the universe, a black hole
wakes, calls out.
We can hear it now,
gravitational waves reaching us
over billions of years in a tiny chirrup,
captured only by fine instruments.

The stars are speaking to each other,
stepping on their thresholds of relativity
in a sway of gravity and time.

The sun spreads across the carpet.
A maple unfolds behind the window.
Pine cones drop on the garden path.

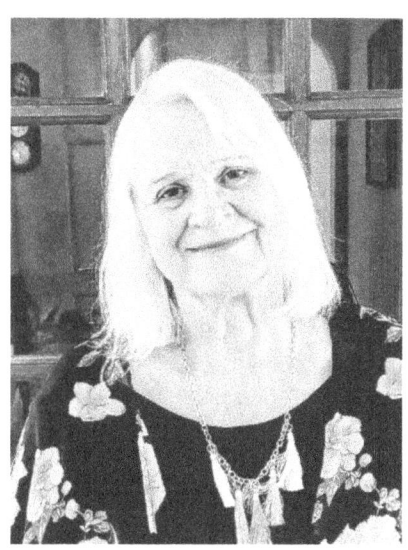

Irene H. Wellman

Irene Wellman is a poet, author, and former teacher of reading. Born in England, she moved to the United States at age 15. She has lived in Africa, New York, Massachusetts, New Hampshire, Virginia, and now in Michigan. She served as associate editor of O.ARS, a poetry journal, in the 1980s. Veteran of many readings, she has been published in journals including *Rattle*, *Artemis*, and *Streetlight*. Her poems have won prizes from The Poetry Society of Virginia. Her chapbook, *In the Space of Time*, was a finalist in the Comstock Review Group Chapbook Contest, 2018.

Her early exposures to Romantic poetry, later to American modernism and postmodernism, and more recently to Japanese aesthetics and philosophy are reflected in her poetry. Her poems also echo her Unitarian Universalist conviction about the connection between spirit and nature.

Irene Wellman is also the author of a middle-grade fantasy/adventure, *The Secret World of Yondhaven* (2021), available on Amazon and Kindle, and from Ash Haven Books 2024 on Facebook.

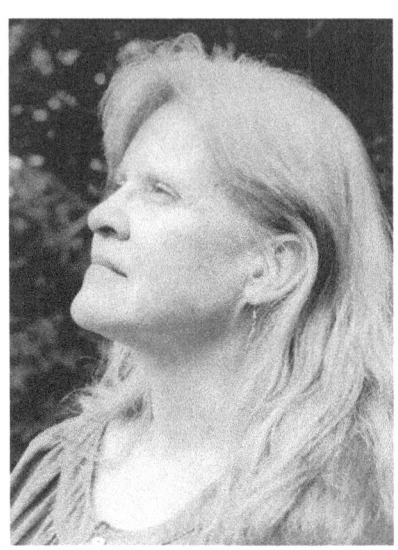

Tara Marvel

Tara Marvel is an author, poet, and artist. She grew up in the White Mountains of New Hampshire and received her BA at the University of Michigan with a major in Asian Art History. In 1969, as a student, she went to Japan and studied printmaking with Tōshi Yoshida. Her study of Asian art and culture over the years led her to practice her own art in a similar form.

When Tara became interested in Native American culture and ceremony, she helped Penobscot elder, Fred Ranco write his autobiography, titled *Muskrat Stew and Other Tales of a Penobscot Life* (2007). Her illustrated poetry chapbook, *Seeking the Tao in the White Mountains*, is available through personal mail. Her joint memoir with Sara Dustin, *Welfare Witches Honorable Mothers* (2024) can be found on *Amazon*.

Tara has published articles, photographs, and illustrations for over 40 years in newspapers, magazines, anthologies, and online. Her video poems have been screened in Spain, France, and the United States. Tara's artwork in this book reflects her ongoing interest in combining Eastern art with a Western vision as revealed by her particular renditions of the five natural elements in this book.